Timely Seasons of Desserts: A Trilogy

Timely Seasons of Desserts: A Trilogy

Poetry by

DARLENE MACHTAN

MACH10 PUBLISHING
RHINELANDER

TIMELY SEASONS OF DESSERTS: A TRILOGY. Copyright © 2020 by Darlene Machtan. All rights reserved. No part of this publication may be reproduced, stored or transmitted in any form or by any means, electronic, mechanical, photocopying, recording, scanning, or otherwise without written permission from the publisher. It is illegal to copy this book, post it to a website, or distribute it by any other means without permission.

Published in the United States of America by Mach10 Publishing.

Photograph credits:
Page 1 Decaying clock on the background of old shabby wise books © Tetyana Afanasyeva/Shutterstock.com.
Page 73 Autumn red leaves in the shape of a heart © LilKar/Shutterstock.com.
Pages 81, 100, 114, 130 and Cover © Darlene Machtan.
Page 145 Vector template with fruit cake with cream stylized as chalk drawing on chalkboard © Ennona Gavrilova_Ellina/Shutterstock.com.

Book design and indexes by Nan Andrews
Publisher caricature by Jim Makris, page 205. Used with permission.

IN THE MIDDLE OF TIME GONE BY: POEMS BY DARLENE MACHTAN. First published in USA by Rhinelander High School, 1988; second printing by Northland Printing, 1998
SEASONS OF A WISCONSIN HEART. First published in USA by Northland Printing, 1994
JUST DESSERTS: POEMS AND RECIPES. First published in USA by Northland Printing, 2001

ISBN 978-1-7344758-5-2 (paperback)
ISBN 978-1-7344758-4-5 (ebook)
Printed in the United States of America
2 4 6 8 10 9 7 5 3 1
This edition reset and published in one volume: April 2020.

Contents

Dedication	xv
Preface	xvi

In The Middle of Time Gone By: Poems by Darlene Machtan (1988)	3
In The Middle of Time Gone By	5
In Appreciation	7
Dedication	9
PART ONE	11
Marriage is a Rugged Country	12
Fall from Grace	13
Evolution	14
Fighting the Wizard of Is	15
Momentum Meets Inertia	16
Telephone Telepathy	18
Seductress Interruptus	19
No Escape	20
Too Expensive	22
Waking Alone at Midnight	23
Two Below Zero	24
Night Shift	26
Re-cycling	27
Knight Errant	28

PART TWO	30
Whatever Happened to the Future Farmers of America?	31
Bill of Sale	32
"Gee, It's Great to Be..."	34
Open Heart	35
Eulogy	36
Auction	37
Weekend Pass	38
Sabotage	40
"Cat's in the Cradle..." (Harry Chapin)	41
PART THREE	42
This Time Yesterday	43
Driver's Education	44
For the Study Lab Boy	45
Monday Blues	46
Mentor	47
Six More Weeks of Winter	48
Double Standards	49
Depth Perception	50
For Laura	51
Euthanasia	52
Piquancy	53
Two for the Price of One	54
Advice to the Adviser	56
PART FOUR	58
Cha lie's Ba 'n Grill	59
Hell	60
Fires that Rage	61
Write a Dream	62

Sex in the '80s	63
Vicious Circle	64
Art Imitating Life	65
Fish Story	66
Falling Out	67
The American Pastime	68
"As If You Could Kill Time Without Injuring Eternity" (Henry David Thoreau)	70
What I Can't Remember	71

Seasons of a Wisconsin Heart: Poems by Darlene Machtan (1994) — 77

In Appreciation	79
Dedication	81
PART ONE: October Snow	83
Love Poem	84
And They're Not Telling	85
Phenomenon of the Tumorous Bed	86
October Snow	88
Forecast	89
Masterpieces	90
But Is Anybody Listening?	91
Eat My Words	92
Three Years from Retirement	94
But It Will Never Happen to Me	95
Missing You	96
Deluge	97
Timing Is Everything	98

Season of Schizophrenia	99
The Grand Canyon	100
PART TWO: Winter Dreams	102
Winter Dreams	103
Empty	104
The Day After	105
August in January	106
Calendar Girl	107
Time Travel	108
February 14, 2142	109
Lost Inside Yesterday	110
Over Easy	111
Dealing With It	112
Grave Robbery	113
Snow Ball	114
PART THREE: Waiting for the Season to Change	116
Rescue	117
Aufwiedersehen?	118
Rules Were Made to Be	119
Tourists that Maim	120
Waiting for the Season to Change	121
In Contempt?	122
Puppy Love	124
Behind the Clouds	125
Wisdom of an Unborn Child	126
When a Friend is a Friend	127
Start Your Engine?	128
Last Song of Spring	129
Manhattan Diagram	130
PART FOUR: The Summer of Fathers	132

Departure	133
Escaping Oz	134
Setting Sail	135
Metaphor	136
Things My Father Taught Me	137
Cinderella	138
Second	139
Machtan's Corollary to Murphy's Law	140
Empathy	141
The Summer of Fathers	142
It Begins August First	144
Cheek to Cheek	145

Just Desserts: A Delightful Mixture of Poems and Recipes by Darlene Machtan (2001)	149
In Appreciation	151
Food For Thought	153
Chocolate Covered Cherries	154
A Little Wind	155
Bon Bons	156
And Now a Word From Your Sponsor	157
Rocky Road Fudge Bars	158
Lemon Bars	160
Answering the Reproaches	161
Basic Sweet Rolls Recipe	162
Carrot Cake	164
As September Leaves / Galaxy	165
Frosted Pineapple Squares	166

A Wish and a Prayer	167
Pie Crust/Blackberry Pie	168
Berry Picking Primer	169
Sugar Cookies	170
Big Wheel of Love	171
Wedding Cake Frosting	172
But Aren't You Married?	173
Blond Brownies	174
Full Circle	175
Molasses Sugar Cookies	176
So Far Away	177
Lemon JELL-O® Gelatin Cake	178
Gone to the Dogs	179
Pecan Puffs	180
Halfway There	181
Raspberry Truffles	182
Historian	183
Ting A Lings	184
Intolerance	185
Cherry Walnut Coffee Cake	186
Butterscotch Supreme Dessert	188
Just Desserts	189
Rhubarb Dessert	190
"Lights Out, Uh Huh—Flash, Flash, Flash"	191
Chocolate Bars	192
Paradoxes	193
Chocolate Mayonnaise Cake	194
Prophecy	195
Peanut Butter Balls	196
Reality Check	197

Black Forest Cake	198
September Song	201
Friendship Brownies	202
Ticked Off	203
Sorcery	204
Final Tip	205
Other Books by Darlene Machtan	207
About the Author	208
Title Index	210
Recipe Index	213

Dedication

For Nan Andrews,
a dear friend of many, many years
whose expertise and encouragement
brought these three books
back to life

Preface

It is Easter Sunday, April 12, 2020. Wisconsin has been under the Safer at Home Mandate since March 23. Schools and churches are closed, along with all non-essential businesses and services. Every U.S. state has declared a state of national emergency. As of today the U.S. has surpassed every other country in the world in COVID-19 related deaths. People are constantly urged to social distance, stand apart a minimum of six feet, avoid gatherings of more than ten, wear face masks, wash hands, wash hands, and wash hands. Video chats and curbside deliveries are a way of life. Hugs and handshakes are nearly forgotten. Thus far, there is no end in sight. These are strange times indeed.

Prior to all this happening, I was looking forward to a publicity and reading/signing blitz for my just-released memoir, *Daddy's Long Goodbye*. I had struggled for over six years to complete it, so I was anxious to get it into circulation. Sadly, to date, that has yet to happen. Perhaps the world will return to some sort of normalcy by Father's Day, a fitting time to promote and share this story of Daddy's and my final journey together.

Finding myself isolated at home with plenty of time and no inclination to do spring cleaning, my mind turned to a writing project I had thought about for years but never gotten around to. I had self-published three chapbooks of poetry between 1988 and 2001 which had been well-received but were long out of print. How about an anthology of all three, I asked my trusty publishing expert Nan Andrews. "Sure," she said, "but the platform we're using will not be available to us anymore after April 30. Can we get it finished in thirty days?"

"What do you think?" I countered.

"I think we can," she said.

We are almost there. I am confident you are holding the results in your hands. I hope you find as much delight reading these pieces for the first time as I found pleasure in revisiting them. This trilogy was not just a labor of love, but one of staying sane and focused in a very scary time in our history. Wishing you health and happiness and sweet delights always,

Darlene

In The Middle of Time Gone By: Poems by Darlene Machtan (1988)

In The Middle of Time Gone By

Here in the middle of time gone by
the young bird stretches,
the young bird flies
East to the ocean,
to the end of the moon
Don't hold to the feathers
You're left with a plume

Yesterday's over, nobody stayed
Gone are the patterns
of yellow and gray
I leave with my taking,
I take what you leave
Roses are petals
we lose and we grieve

Did you see me last summer
Did you follow me home
Did you read the illusion
I called it a poem
Tomorrow's horizon's
unfettered and free
I ask for your sympathy
Lend it to me

Because it's on to the east
where the moon meets the sun
When time runs amuck
but the striving goes on
Goodbye to the fledgling,
goodbye to the nest
goodbye to the past
and hello to the rest

In Appreciation

This book would not have been possible without the help of my friends and colleagues.

First, thanks to my readers Julie Bronson, Marie Martini, and John Fortier who waded through my original manuscript, helping me cull the good from the bad and offering their encouragement to actually go ahead with this publication.

Secondly, thanks to Robin Mills, Bob Nash, and Dan Jalinski for their computer, printing, and binding expertise. The many hours they contributed to this book are visible with the turn of every page.

Lastly, thanks to Michael, who never once doubted that this book would become a reality, and who first made me think of myself as a poet.

Dedication

**For my mother,
a woman whose strength
and love
will endure
forever**

PART ONE

Marriage is a Rugged Country

Marriage is a Rugged Country

You can't always tell
the cowboys from the Indians
sometimes it's me
who wields the tomahawk
sometimes it's you
Infidelity wages war
against faith
on the frontier of peace of mind
You can circle
the wedding band
all you want
and still feel the arrow
piercing the heart
In the end there are no Indians at all,
just two black hats
in the classic tradition
facing off in a dusty street:
compromise
or gun each other down

Fall from Grace

Stepped on your
fingertips clinging to the edge
Didn't mean to
Didn't see you there
Forgot to watch
where I was walking
Forgot about the drop from high
to nothingness
Can't undo it
but I'm reaching out both hands
to help you up again
God, I'm sorry
Will you trust me to tread carefully
next time
you are clinging to the edge?

Evolution

I was looking for a prince
the day I ran into a
red-haired frog
"Kiss me," he croaked.
Afraid of warts
and the spread of disease
I declined.
He was less than I'd dreamed of
and he walked funny.
But it was a slow weekend,
and even an amphibian
had some appeal.
We went for a ride–
Turned out his hands weren't slippery
and his warm blue eyes
were worth swimming in
Strange how as the night went on
he transformed
Strange how years later
he keeps getting better
Wonder what will happen
when we finally kiss.

Fighting the Wizard of Is

I spent all last night
not escaping his bed
Merlin's sorcery
let him freeze me
What's wrong, honey
every time
I tried to run away

You can't fix it
if it isn't broken
Oh, Lady, why shatter it
just to see if you can

If only he would give me
reason to hate him
Provoke me to slice away
habits that won't bleed

If only I were not
at so much ease
with one love
standing in the way
of yet another
who offers nothing

The spell of contentment
battles against
darker charms
and every night
knows just how much it costs
to stay the dragon

Momentum Meets Inertia

An immovable object (him)
meets an unstoppable force (me)
Ka-pow!!!
Put up the curtain rods, Dear
Sure–Sunday
Put up the curtain rods tonight
Maybe Saturday
Put up the curtain rods NOW
or
(the ultimate threat)
I'll do it myself

Uncontrolled chortling
You? Use a screwdriver??
It is to laugh.
OK–forget the screwdriver–
gimme a hammer.
DON'T use a hammer–I told you
nails pull out
Then you put up the curtain rods NOW!!!
I'm tired. Maybe Sunday.

OK, that's it.
You know that sleeping bag
you said you'd put away last Sunday?
(this punctuated by a thundering ascent to the loft)
It's STILL draped over the railing.
Oops–not anymore–
I just knocked it over the edge
Sorry–it was an accident.

Oh really–
two can play that little game.
You know that stupid afghan
you strategically draped

next to my sleeping bag?
Oops–
sorry–
it was an accident.

Pick it up, you jerk–
that took me months to crochet!
Pick it up!!
Sorry, honey, I lost my head–
but so did you.
OK, I'm sorry too.
Put the curtain rods up now?
Nah....
maybe Sunday

Telephone Telepathy

Willing the phone to ring
Call, damn it
Staring across the room
at silence across the miles
Visualize
him picking up the phone
dialing a dormant number
bridging much too long distance
with an unexpected expected hello
Thirty thousand lifetimes
since the last conversation
growing older with every silent night
willing the phone to ring
Call, damn it

Seductress Interruptus

Never did
but I thought about it
and I've been trying
ever since
to remember to forget

Who could have blamed me
really–except everybody
Just because
it was only partly wrong
didn't make it all right

I feel so responsbile
because I wasn't
because it ended
but it didn't

Are your eyes still green
or were those mine
and do you never
find yourself
listening to the radio
trying to remember
to forget?

No Escape

Out into the night
just to walk
just to breathe clean air again
All these feelings
need
betrayal
Walk it off.
Walk it off.
Moonlight forgives and promises
more than he could. Than he did.
Doesn't hold me anymore
when he sees the need
within my eyes–
only when they're empty.
Doesn't tell me any secrets
and I stopped telling mine
a long time ago
Walk it off.
Walk it off.
Away from something old
Away from something new
Too soon to borrow a new love's tears
Such a long time blue.
Night time road
unexpected twists
of the ankle
of the mind
Shimmering water soothes as it
whispers
advises me
to walk it off, walk it off.
I could walk along forever
head away, head held high
Take my time with my leaving
slowly move to the edge
But the anger and the hurt

and the love
linger and burn
and I could walk away,
but I could never walk it off.

Too Expensive

The day she finally
read the phone bill
was the day she learned
he'd been unfaithful
Looking back
she'd known it all along really
Milwaukee weekends
he made sure she couldn't find him
late night calls she answered
to hear only nervous breathing
new cologne for no apparent reason
silence deafening her ears
And then the phone bill
and all those calls
to the same Lake Geneva exchange

She should have left him, of course
Confronted him and then walked
but there was the house
the business
losing everything
to indiscretion.
All over a phone bill?
Forgiveness didn't come easy
and she never ever did forget.
She blamed it all on GTE.
Long distance–
the next best thing to being there.

Waking Alone at Midnight

Under the wait of quilts
straining for
the sound of your breathing
I drown in fear
What if you never come home?
What if you lie crushed
or frozen in the moonlight?
Insistent refusal
gives way to fantasy
the phone call
the funeral
the emptiness
insurance
independence
unfettered choices
Under the wait of quilts
gentled by inner strength
I drown in options
until the key in the lock
the accustomed footfall
cements us together again

Two Below Zero

Two below zero, two below par
You've wondered too lately,
you've wandered too far
Walked out of my half light
into your night
We're two below might have been
Colder than white

Spring found us warming
our hands in a fire
with each passing minute
it burned ever higher
Too hot not to handle
Too hot not to touch
A raging inferno–
but never too much

Summer we mellowed
a bit by the sea
burns were relieved
and soothed by the breeze
Sand warmed our bodies
our fingers and toes
We welcomed the embers
instead of hot coals

Fall found you drifting
It brought a new chill
Winds howled evenings
down from the hill
Only the nights
when you needed some heat
brought you here next to me
under my sheet

And winter is empty,
the snow piles higher
Frozen and snowed in,
I call you a liar

The fires you promised
have all gone to dust
and nothing is left here
nothing but us

and we're two below zero
two below par
You've wondered too lately,
you've wandered too far
Walked out of my half light
into your night
We're two below might have been
Colder than white

Night Shift

Why don't you come
to bed with me?
We could cuddle and
tell secrets

No–I'm standing guard
like the watcher
in prehistoric days
like the young adult male baboon
in the animal kingdom
Watching–for what?
For attackers–for killers–
for interlopers–
Go to sleep–don't worry
I'll be watching.

Ha ha–a ploy
Help! HELP! There's a
murderer in this bedroom!!
I'm serious!! Help! Help!
No answer.
Help! Help!
No answer.
Sleepiness
settling in. Snuggling down.
help help
Sleepier still...help...help
A sudden movement
and then warmth
Snapping awake
WHO IS IT?

Just the big bad wolf,
Little Girl, just the watcher.

Re-cycling

The daughter that I plan
to never have
is named Katherine
On days I love her most
I call her Kitty

Her wry wisdom
pricks my sensiblity
"Maybe you have to have me
to want me,"
she whispers in the wind

She grows up
tall and strong and beautiful
willow-rooted
deep and bending/binding
cool haven on midnight Augusts
soothing my feverish run from winter

How gently she dries my fears
and how I miss her
on days I love her most
I call her Kitty

Knight Errant

Through all my crusades
you have stood and stand beside me
ready to disarm the enemy
within and without
Tarnished armor
still gleams when it needs to
You have slain my
dragons of despair more than once
and when they rise up again
to engulf me
you will quell the flames

I overlook your imperfections
in my need to be defended
and so do you
Your lady longer
than any of the others,
I huddle snug inside your fortress
warm against the winds
of middle ages

PART TWO

Whatever Happened to the Future Farmers of America?

Whatever Happened to the Future Farmers of America?

Last weekend
driving down broken asphalt
I saw faded red barns
splintering into oblivion,
once-farmers wandering
from leafless tree to tree
death blowing past them
as they shuffled along
Old
everything and everybody
bent by time
Nothing growing anywhere at all
Green gone from the spectrum
along with Holsteins and
Durocs and Suffolks

Oh, but see the
Milwaukee doctors'
quarter horses glimmering
outside manicured stables

I wonder
Who is left
to feed America?

Bill of Sale

You're buying my folks' farm
It's a package deal, you know
You get the buttercups
that bloom lush and wild
along the creek every spring
and the nettle
that stingingly embraces
each attempt to pick them
The branches of the mountain ash
we swung high enough from
to learn the fear of falling
shade nothing now
but still you will have
to mow around the stump

You get mammoth stone monuments
to wonder at
but you won't feel hands
encased in dirt
nose cindered
from a day of casting rocks up high
in the annual purge
You get the pastures
and the sagging fences
but not the mending walks
my father and I took
to secure them and him and me
back up again

You get the field behind the barn
and in it a rotted partial plate
we never found when Ken laughed it out
one dusky evening we raced home

I'm sorry about the straw mow floor
but at seven I had the notion
there was buried treasure
under those boards

They stopped me after I pried
the fourth one loose
I nailed them down again
but they never were the same

The hardwood floors in the house
are solid, though
We skated across them in our socks
after she waxed
If you pull up the too-modern carpet
you will see
the shadows of my footprints
somewhere there

The rain won't always come
and the crops won't always grow
at least not like the fertilizer man
says they will
The seasons will be too long
and too short
and the work will never end
You won't ever be able to walk away
from the sixteen hour days
and when the time finally comes
to pass it on to someone else
the letting go will be harder than
all the bad weeks put together
It's a package deal

"Gee, It's Great to Be..."

Back home on a Sunday
to mourn the sale of
childhood
Room to room I drift
taking 35 mm pictures
of my past
How small and worn it's all become
in its emptiness
The shutter's clicking echoes
against fresh-painted walls
attempts to cover
penciled marks of growing

Out into March winds
I seek the solace of
the cathedral-ceilinged haymow
someone else's sunbeams
streaming through the boards
that house someone else's hay
Steady now–
catch that shaft of light just so–
picture perfect–
perfect enough to last forever
because this is the last Sunday
I will ever be back home

Open Heart

The day she had
quadruple by-pass surgery
Daddy didn't see
why he needed to be there
two brothers said they had to work
a third was off at college
the fourth I'd already lost to death
and now it was my mama

The day she had
quadruple by-pass surgery
you sat beside me watching
while I crocheted
a perfectly dreadful afghan
even asked for the pattern
After nine hours and seventeen minutes
you walked me to recovery
reassured me
then drove me home

Doctors patched
my mother's broken heart
and sent her back to me
but just like always
you were the one
who mended mine

Eulogy

Tragic
for a man to die
at twenty-four
with a wife
and three children
dependent upon him
Strange
that this family,
not regular members
of this church,
coming only at Christmas,
if then,
should have had three deaths
in less than one month
But God does not punish
Perhaps the demise of
this young man–
what was his name?–
is a warning
a reminder
that the church demands
regular attendance
total commitment
Do not grieve
for his widow or his children
but change your own attitude
lest your widow and children
be the ones who grieve
But always remember–
God does not punish.
Find comfort in that.
Amen.

Auction

They came to bid
on pieces
of my father's hands,
my mother's heart

Only the bitter March wind
that blew them raw
seemed to understand
they had no right

Weekend Pass

Tired Kansas USO club
1943
I am a woman whose
intelligent young face
will belong to a daughter
in forty years

Starched Air Corps suntans
have fallen limp
in one hundred and three degrees

My darting gray eyes
see your wire rims
glint across the room
They separate you from the rest
Much in contrast to me
you are
angular
well-muscled
thin
sure of of your small talk
generating raucous laughter

I wonder if you see
my shadowed pool of silence

"In the Mood"
and you extend
your snapping fingers
swaying hips
to me

I slide a ping-pong paddle
in between us
I am sure of ping-pong
I can beat your thirty ways
on any given Sunday

You will marry me for that precision
and that spirit
but I will never dance
Forty years of careful deftness
will become my trademark
and still you will be
seeking out
a partner

Sabotage

Tommy
best friend of my older brother
26 to 20
I didn't stand a chance, he figured
Between engagements
he'd steal kisses
in the kitchen
With Tommy,
everything was burning
Finally he asked me
and I said yes
My sister-in-law gasped
"You're going out with that
sleazebag?
He's fast; he's really fast.
Be careful."
I laughed, red-faced
It's just a date, I said
Movie wasn't long enough
Popcorn wasn't greasy enough
to slow Tommy down
Your apartment? he asked.
I don't think so–
Not tonight, I sputtered
He followed me in anyway
Poor Tommy
whining and pleading
using all those worn-out lines
It took every
counter-commando move
my brothers had taught me
just to keep
from upping his body count
Defeated he slunk out the door
into the cold arms of darkness
The last time I saw him,
of course
It was almost worth it

"Cat's in the Cradle..." (Harry Chapin)

Fathers and sons
separate
and die alone
Mothers and daughters
unite
and live together
My mother's eyes
dart along my lifeline
her piercing blue-gray
housed in my face
under her brows
And behind them
her values, expectations, guilt
My father is
the one you hear
when teasing one-liners
slide between my lips
but it is my mother's ambition
that assaults me
and it is her jaw
that I set in grim determination
as I forge ahead.
She will live forever.
Even now
I see
my mother's hands
busily shaping
each unsuspecting you

PART THREE

This Time Yesterday

This Time Yesterday

Somebody said they'd hire me
ten years ago
and I've been doing time
ever since
These halls are filled
with ghosts of past prisoners
who've graduated to
other levels of despair

They were in for various crimes–
insolence, immaturity, apathy
They sawed through
invisible bars on the windows
plotted their inevitable escapes
I hear Ann Panko is
busting out in June
She's excited
so she's rubbing it in

I will still be incarcerated
come September–
but I'm comfortable
with the lifetime sentence–
so familiar am I with
the cells and inmates

Ann Panko's busting out
in June to
white freedom
endless space
and empty faces
Is she frightened yet?
Does she know she ought to be?

Driver's Education

He was
my driver's ed teacher
It was
the first day of class
I was
fifteen and frightened
Driving scared me.
Driving made people die.
He said,
"Some of you
think you don't need this class."
He said,
"Some of you
think you already know how to drive.
Like that Machtan kid," he said.
"He thought he knew how to drive.
Ended up dead–
got drunk and tried to
outrun the cops.
A culvert stopped him.
Yeah, he thought he knew
how to drive.
He was wrong."
They were
all staring at me.
They were
all watching me cry.
That Machtan
kid was my brother
and a year before to the day
we'd buried him.
He was never coming back
but I had to
every lousy, broken day
to learn to drive

For the Study Lab Boy

Nobody worked harder
to get out alive
Hours and hours just getting it write
God, I admired your zest
and your drive–
the way that you put up the fight

Spelling the demons
and splicing the frags
trying to order
the chaos of thought
Nobody ever needed so much
or listened so well when I taught

I am so happy that you're moving on
but I'm sad
that you're leaving me here
where nobody's eyes
will be quite as bright
when September earmarks a new year.

Seeing you there
in that cap and that gown
Nobody ever deserved it so much
Now that you're out there
alone on your own
Try not to fall out of touch

Monday Blues

On Monday
the sun belongs
to other people
You know the ones–
sidewalk mothers
pulling gurgling toddlers
in little red wagons,
lawyers in three-piece gray
on their way
to cocktail lunches
at the Pub,
retirees in broad-brimmed straw
clipping back
couldn't reach grass
spear by spear

On Monday
the sun belongs to other people
but not to us
locked insde
fluorescent institution green
daydreaming out of streaked windows
willing the clock hands
to inch their way
to 3 p.m. freedom
which sadly
and usually
is cloudy

On Monday
the sun belongs
to other people

Mentor

It took a while
for us to see
that flowers and ferns
belong together
Roses or daffodils
carnations or daisies
are lost without
the brilliant feathered green
of contrast
All flower/all fern:
an empty vase
of too-much-not-enough

Already we miss
the desktop tributes
to the differences–
sporadic thanks you's
in the guise of just because
In the fall we see an empty space
of flowers, but no fern,
and we wish we hadn't taken
quite so long
to learn the lesson

Six More Weeks of Winter

Sunshine
filters through the
window of my mind
casting shadows of
a boy who used to be
I saw you walking down
the hall again today
black curls flecked with silver
over the upturned parka collar
the tilt of your head
your lonely stance
You've been gone since forever
but I'm still
standing where you stood
casting shadows of a boy
who used to be

Double Standards

They're thinking for themselves
Ain't it a shame
They want a voice
take part of the blame

We've taught 'em to question
stand up for their rights
yet now that they're speaking
it's out go the lights

Shut up and sit down, kid
Play by our rules
You'll do what we tell ya
at least here in school

Now back to the lesson
of freedom of speech–
but I don't expect you
to live what I preach

Depth Perception

It's too close
you halfway across the room
looking back at me
with green eyes I can barely see
but know are crinkled in amusement
It's too close
I can see behind
thick curls I have counted
and know you think
to yourself
she swears at will
she tells nasty jokes
she doesn't drink at all
of fornicate outside of marriage
but she thinks about it
It's too close
You know far too much
about my wishes and lies
to buy the current image
I am selling
There is not distance enough
between us
for your perception
to be clouded
but there is too much space
for me to be the one
you really know

For Laura

Not always easy
to be the one that
listens
Not always hard
to just walk away
But you're still bending
in the breeze
and so is she

Gentleness becomes you
Like pussy willows
you are strong and welcome
in her life of endless winters
broken promises
tumultuous dreams
People like Melissa depend upon
strong harbingers of spring
People like you depend upon her need
The world is full
of harsh reds and greens
but the patches
of gentle velvet gray
are rarer and warmer
and as for me,
I'll take pussy willows
over geraniums
any day

Euthanasia

The always bruised child
towers over
her shriveled father
electronic tubes
transport his very air
sputtering
he chokes out
his apology
sorries for
a thousand blackened eyes
she sees
he cannot help his lying
she sees that he is
desperate to die
Flick the switch
You always wanted to
You dreamed of
death with every beating
He wants it
He's begging
just like you did
Let him die
Let him die
Go on,
let him die
No,
no.
For his sins
make him live

Piquancy

Woman in a scarlet dress
fingers the black snake
cinched around her waist
wonders how it felt
to swallow fifty-one pills
to stop the pounding
wonders how it feels
to have the throat constrict
even at the thought
of aspirin now
wonders if his heart
speeds or slows
at the magnitude of the deed
the echoing near-loss
the hurt in her eyes

Woman in a scarlet dress
accepts the need
to turn some heads
fly a little near the sun
anticipate resounding thunder
with a self-imposed flash
of lightning
understands the sizzle of contrast–
ebony and red
suicide and kings–
but she wonders if sensation
is always worth the scandal
or if this time
provocative didn't have
one dimension
too many

Two for the Price of One

Kansas, 1968
Danny Petrie, solid and strong
He liked workin' on cars
bein' outside
and me
Liked me so much that he
taught me how
to use an impact wrench
took me ridin' on his cycle
at twilight
Kansas, 1975
Danny Petrie, warm and wonderful
He liked 3.2 beer
a new yellow Cougar
and me
Liked me so much he
drove me two hundred miles
to the Wichita airport,
wanted me to be
his best man

Wisconsin, what seems like yesterday
Danny Bruso, solid and strong
He liked workin' on cars
bein' outside
and me
Liked me so much that he
took all my classes,
rendezvoused in printing
RHS, just last semester
Danny Bruso, warm and wonderful
He liked Budweiser beer
a maroon Nova
and me
Liked me so much he
gave me homemade angel food,
M&M'S for early graduation

February, 1986
Everything is lost
and Danny Petrie, Danny Bruso
come to the rescue
A Bible and vase
from the cousin–
his faith and outdoor love
passed on to me
Moral support and muscle
from the student
moving soot-covered metal out
too-new appliances in

The ash settles
and I see
the not-so-distant past
linked to the ever-present
I count my double blessings
I count on both of you

Advice to the Adviser

There you stood
your silvery suave essence
oozing charm and
promises of immortality
Singling me out
cemented my past
to your present
elevated me to demagogue
disciple of the Buddha–
an illusion
like your name
initials that seem to stand
for nothing
You single-handedly committed
a college junior to teaching
I live in Room 214
because you pointed in this direction
Don't you want to know
what happened?
Don't you wonder
how it all came out?
The good ol' boy nodded and smiled
as he handshook his way past me
but he never paused
to assess what he accomplished
ask me how I felt
I am enraged
that ten years ago
I embraced your plan for my future
and ten years later
you do not even care enough
to embrace

Cha lie's Ba 'n Grill and Other Unrelated Poems

Cha lie's Ba 'n Grill

An American greasy spoon
with Chinese flair
Holes where absent r's
disappeared in blinking neon
Lifetimes got sucked
into those cavities
Dying men drowned in
their half-filled coffee cups
Aging waitresses
counted on tomorrow
for the big tipper
Cha-lie had been gone
since nobody could remember,
and nobody wondered why
but everybody
guessed it wouldn't be long
'til the sign went out
forever

Hell

Bone-chilling
Satan's icy breath
freezes thought, free will
Numb for eternity
in a room
with a reborn Christian
whose zealous fervor
didn't save her
On she preaches
Son of God, Son of God, Son of God
Never were
yellow rays of hope
never will be
Every day is a cold day in hell
where a second is a season of forever
and spring is doomed
to never come at all

Fires that Rage

Hold out your hand
and close your eyes
and you will feel
your fingers fry

Blisters bubble
and raise in degrees
while those who offend me
are brought to their knees

Sizzles of flesh
filling the air
the sweetest aroma
of freshly singed hair

Oh stop all your moaning
and don't waste your tears
When you burn me up
I keep burning for years

Write a Dream

I did not go to class
not once
in an entire semester
but here I am
and everything depends
upon this final test
I cannot read the questions
I see each letter
but the logic blurs
from word to word
Everyone around me
is competently writing
filling blue books with
what is obvious to them
I did not go to class
I cannot read the questions
How could I let this happen?
Frustration, terror
My eyes widen
Tears threaten
to flood away what is left
of my dignity
and I am horrified to discover
I am
my own
worst student

Sex in the '80s

Ain't she sweet
bet she plays
between the sheets
Blue eyes swimmin'
with desire and heat
Ain't she sweet

Ain't he hot
Bet he's proud
of what he's got
He gets around
and he gets a lot
Ain't he hot

Ain't they dead
Looked for love–
caught AIDS instead
"Disease claims two"
is what the paper said
Ain't they dead

Vicious Circle

Chocolate is my passion
A prostitute for M&M'S
Another hour of aerobics
just to savor the sweetness

A prostitute for M&M'S
I sweat to feed my habit
Just to savor the sweetness
pumping iron for my sins

I sweat to feed my habit
Five pounds to lose and gain
pumping iron for my sins
and then a hot fudge sundae

Five pounds to lose and gain
Chocolate is my passion
and then a hot fudge sundae
another hour of aerobics

Art Imitating Life

Art doesn't breathe
and art doesn't weep
It never gets old
and it never sleeps

It's never ill-tempered
It never gives in
It never complains
about where it's been

It doesn't have children
or spouses who cheat
It's never a victim
of crime in the street

No art isn't life
and it's better than way
or museums would sicken us
all every day

Fish Story

Sun setting rainbows
on Arctic water
ringing circles into moonlight
Last catch of the day
so cold I can hardly stand
to touch the
slippery northern fight
for flight
One final slice towards freedom,
then up and out and in

My hands argue with him
dying to live
So dark now I can hardly see
him grimace
but I know those razors
do not smile
Gingerly I feel two barbs
work my way around the third
meet resistance and
with a scraping set
the daredevil free.

He flops again; his eyes,
all that reflect the fading light,
wink up at me.
It would be so easy, he says

A piercing movement through water
that closes faster
than the twilight
His laughter echoes

Falling Out

Dear Tom,

Thinking of you
lately
your hairy chest
mustache
and giggle
I once thought
you were
irreplaceable
thought no one
could ever make
my heart skip
your way
But there has been
a string of others
Sam Elliott
Ted Danson
even too-short
Huey without the News
You were good, Tom,
but just not good enough
to stay in my Nielsen ratings
forever.
It's over, sweetheart,
I'm sorry, Mr. Selleck,
but you've been
cancelled.

No love,

Your once ardent admirer

The American Pastime

Men and women, old and young,
live for the game
and the game's begun
You know how it is
when she gives you that look
and nothing's accomplished
if you play by the book

A little flirtation,
a lot with the eyes
Violating promises
made 'til you die
Walk over there, babe,
he'll tell you the rules
and as long as you're cheating,
do it with fools

Buy her a drink,
light up her cig
Tell her that outfit
is one that you dig
Ask her to dance
when the music is slow
Whisper the question,
how far can you go

Agree to go with him,
pretend it's all new
You know he believes
it's not something you do
every Friday and Saturday night
but it's been several years
since you've worn any white

And it just doesn't matter
who scores in the end
There aren't any losers
when everyone bends

The American pastime
for red-blooded boys
with red-blooded women
for red-blooded toys

"As If You Could Kill Time Without Injuring Eternity" (Henry David Thoreau)

Time doesn't fly
She limps along
on peg leg moments
(most of them gone)

Wasted hours
bleeding the day
maiming forever
as she lurches away

Seconds are dying
minutes are dead
adding up to a lifetime
of lives never led

Wounded tomorrows
exhumed yesterdays...
for the killing of time
the murderer pays

What I Can't Remember

Phone numbers
addresses
faces and names
Prices and
totals
and who was to blame
Bittersweet
evenings just
as they were
How long I've
waited
to be really sure
Directions
that tell
how to
get back again
Where I have
hidden
a number of friends
Days that I
said I would
never forget
The fact that
the rain leaves you
lonely and wet

Seasons of a Wisconsin Heart: Poems by Darlene Machtan (1994)

In Appreciation

With the encouragement of friends, in 1988 I published *In the Middle of Time Gone By*. That book is sold out now, but people are still asking for it. Rather than reprint it, I decided to generate something new. I could not have managed this undertaking without the help and guidance of my friends and colleagues.

Thank you to my readers Julie Bronson, Marie Martini, Nan Andrews, and Bob Owens for helping me separate the wheat from the chaff. A special thanks to Bob Owens who spotted the common denominator in the poems which provided the framework for the book.

Finally, thanks to Homer, who said, "Yours is as good as any that's out there." And meant it.

Dedication

This one's
for my father,
the grinning other half
of who I am

and in fond memory
of Karin Haissig,
who was herself
a poem

PART ONE: October Snow

Love Poem

Sirens race the heart
and shorten breath
Every time's the first time
I kissed Mr. Death

Twisted metal scars
leaving blood and tears
I still miss my brother
after all these years

And They're Not Telling

I guess they had landed on the river
When I saw them
they were headed south again,
laughing at the disarray
of starting over.
I stopped to watch
them writing eagerly
to order chaos.
Not recognizable
as any letter of the alphabet,
they scripted their way
across a patternless gray.
A logic emerged as
stragglers surged forward
while the leaders eased
until an I formed,
and then a Y,
and then a V.
I sighed.
How is it
that they know
exactly
where they're going
and how to get there
with such style
and grace
and song?

Phenomenon of the Tumorous Bed

Only a twin
the last morning
arms and legs entangled
in space far less than enough
for one
Breathing in tandem
just to conserve
room and oxygen
Nearly suffocating
and for what?

Full
the first nights
nothing but mattress
head to toe
Closest thing to
an unwanted man
was a self-sought Charlie horse
thundering over the rise
of indulgent stretching

Queen
by Friday
Nobody to answer to
except an absent king
but the royal chamber
echoed loud enough
to frighten dreams

This morning I awoke
lost in Siberia
huddled and frigid
Even all your blankets
could not warm me
Ice is forming
well past

used-to-be edges
I am terrified of
what lost continent
tonight will bring
Hurry home?

October Snow

It falls gently
Like what–
not tears, exactly–
it's lighter than that
Not expectation–
it's whiter than that
Not aging muscle–
it's tighter than that
Not loosened morals–
it's righter than that

It falls gently
but appears to never land
something quite uncommon
for the all-too-common man

Forecast

It must be time
for a phone call
or visit
because it's raining
and dark
which it always is
when you arrive/leave
Almost a year
since your eyes waved so long
maybe for good
maybe for bad
I hardly ever
wonder how you are
anymore
or where you went
or why
No, I never think of you at all
except some sunless, moonless moments
like today
when I'm raining

Masterpieces

Paint me October
I said
wild winds
flailing branches
passion to gaze at
all year long
But he never did
fearing failure
or worse
success
which would change everything
Last night
we brushed
five hours
of October together
Like daVinci
we were careless
about the paint
Everything faded by morning–
even the wind disappeared

But Is Anybody Listening?

Under the
carefully shredded jeans
and the Slayer t-shirt
under the hairspray
and iridescent eye shadow
under the attitude of
nothin' means
nothin' to me
and you can't make it,
someone whispers
someone whispers
a poem

Eat My Words

8:30 a.m. ringing
interrupts
quilted sniffles
I lost your directions
she apologizes
I've never done this before
Some kid must have taken them
Had 'em, but they disappeared
O.K., I croak wearily, take this down...

Next day
no one knows anything
the picture of innocence
when I mention it
"Spastic Sub Disease"
the only explanation
until...

Next next day
parent snags me
in the mall
laughs and says
He ate them up!!
Excuse me–?
Your sub instructions–
that boy took them and
ate them
my daughter said

Oh God
impossible
but such a credible source

Next next next day
The Inquisition
Spencer ate them
No one knows if he
swallowed them

or spit them out
but they saw them
disappear
inside his ever open mouth

I always knew it
Poor Spence–
so very, very hungry
for knowledge

Three Years from Retirement

Just like I never left
orange and yellow
straight-backed rows
uncertain silence
pens moving-not moving
unsteadily across blank pages
Jeans and t-shirts change
but they don't
Some kids old
Some kids new
Borrowed trouble
Back and blue
They come and go
I go and come
Another year
of rechewed gum

But It Will Never Happen to Me

We live on the edge of black ice
but we can't see it
Underfoot we feel
terra firma
and believe holy
souly in certain
Sons, mothers
fathers and lovers
we take for granted
until sudden freezing rain
and the slightest mistake
fishtail us away
forever

Missing You

A shadow lingers
on the face of the moon
It's darker earlier
and longer
since you left me
Nights wait for a lonely me
while I wait for you
The clock ticks louder
Rain is colder
I grow tired
I grow older
My face empties
without your eyes
An oxymoron–
this goodbye

Deluge

Goodbye torrent roaring
inside my rushing mind
Acid tears like rivers
burn gorges as they wind
Why if it's the right thing
does it feel like dying?
Why if I must have restraint
can't I stop this crying?
Must I be the remnants
hurried to the end?
Damn these flooding waters
Let's begin again

Timing Is Everything

I am the chrysanthemum
I bought eight years ago
to hold onto Mexico
Its lush foliage
spills over and around
the sides of the whiskey barrel
that fail to enclose it
laden with blossoms
liked closed eyes of God
It laughs at the calendar
November 6 and still it chooses
not to bloom
One real frost
should have reduced it
to black slime
but several snows later
it's still grinning
tall and green

Every day I check to see
if it has finally agreed to flower
I tell myself
if it blooms before it dies
so will I
My future is somehow linked
to a plant
that started too late
to take its responsibilities seriously
Two days of Indian summer
and we'd both be home free
but I fear another cold front's
moving in

Season of Schizophrenia

Blizzards the first of November
Zero two days after that
Fifty and melting the thirteenth
Why am I wearing this hat?

All winter and spring in the same month
Summer may show up next week
Wisconsin plays by its own rules
of seasonal hide-and-go-seek

The Grand Canyon

Looking at you like that
40,000 miles divide us
I don't know you at all
never felt your hand in mine
never kissed you in the moonlight
never told you the truth
about any everything
Looking at me like that
40,000 smiles divide us
You don't know me at all
never danced me into darkness
never led me down the path of dreams
never heard my red laughter
at every anything
Distance today divides and conquers
doubles, dwindles, disappears
Distance today has left us
longing
falling down an edge
of separate years

PART TWO: Winter Dreams

Winter Dreams

W indows of the widow
I lluminate the past
N o one now to hold her
T hrough lonely nights that last
E ven in the arms of night
R ichard's far away

D ying in the emptiness
R ise up and face the day
E verybody knows he's gone
A nd says, "I understand"
M aybe he will come tonight
S o she can sleep again

Empty

Nobody's home
So?
Nobody's knocked
in a long, long time
He is hunting color
but all he sees is gray
above and below
outside and in
When and if
he finally speaks
only he can hear
the whisper
If and when
he pulls the trigger
No sound will echo
only absence
of the absence
of a heartbeat

The Day After

Denied your presence
for another year
Much too soon
to start counting the days
The event doesn't mean anything
anyway you know–
only anticipation
decoration
fascination
and afterwards
crumpled paper
under a tired tree
Still, red foil wrap
lurks in the closet
and an evergreen grows
toward the sun
waiting, waiting
for Christmas

August in January

Cool
moist dark soil cushions
a heaven of
broad green leaves
Sunny silk
rustles in a temperate breeze
Home waits just the other side
of used-to-be
where old cow dogs, reborn
nose past and smile
chasing dreams
No one knows to look
so no one finds me here
crouched inside a summer memory

Calendar Girl

Hold on, hold on
just for a minute
make it stay
Stand still, damn it–
Look at me
long enough for us both
to remember
subzero mornings
February thaws
bitter March winds
elusive April sunbeams
and the promise, the promise
of maybe summer
June twilight
July thunder
Searing August afternoons
give way to September cinnamon
October sighs
November cries
then December lies
wide awake
through the longest night of the year
and all I can do–
all you can do–
is hold on, hold on

Time Travel

Wind blows a dusting of snow
and loose soil into
the cracks of deprivation
No brightly-wrapped packages
this year
but that's OK
There's no balsam to
nestle them under anyway
A family of six
can't afford December 25
in 1932
Even the little ones
somehow understand
that two oranges
to be divided in half
will have to be
Christmas enough

February 14, 2142

I am dead now
longer than I ever was alive
and so are you
No one remembers
our morning secrets
hugs from a too-short man
to a too-tall woman
or that it didn't matter
Light years from lovers
just friends looking out of
and into
the same pair of eyes
I have grown long and lovely
all these years
into an American beauty
and the daughter of your
son's son's son
is blossoming too
She is what is left of you
and I the flower
her first love picks
and hands her with a kiss
History repeats itself
and together we make romance
bloom again

Lost Inside Yesterday

Too much time
spent looking back
looking black
Tired eyes
Tired whys
cloud today
disguise tomorrow
Introspection
change direction
or maybe change
the color of your lies
How and what
are clear enough
but you can never
really figure out
goodbyes

Over Easy

"Why is it
if you speak English
and I speak English
we can't understand each other?"
Carl Sandburg

An empty shell
she sits
fragile
waiting
wanting
to be broken
He told her once
he loved her
but that was before
resignation
replaced her
face of sixteen
before burnt toast
was a regular thing
and the coffee
was just too strong

It wasn't the babies
or always running out of eggs
that cost so much
just the empty sameness
of every day
every night
She sits
fragile
waiting
wanting
to be broken
but he doesn't
even have the
decency
to drop her

Dealing With It

The only thing I knew
was that he
wasn't prepared to see
what I had seen:
thirty years of memory
reduced to still-smoking cinders
A gutted ruin
and nothing would ever
bring it back
All he said
staring straight into the ashes
was
I guess this means that
we'll be
dining out
this evening

Grave Robbery

Ash up to the ankles
a mountain of used-to-be
Neighbors cluck their tongues
Too bad, they say
How much do you have to have
for your firewood?
How'd it start?
Like it matters
like they are thinking
about anything other
than cleaning their chimneys
on the weekend
I'm sorry
Tough break
If there's anything I can do just
Two days later
they stand in what
used to be your bedroom
kicking through
smudged pieces of
your heart
After all,
once the walls burn
anyone can come inside

Snow Ball

Who taught
snowflakes
how to waltz?
They never miss
step on toes
knock knees
So very, very white
patterns in a blacker universe
gentle coldness
tiny unconnected parts
She joins
her hand with one
dissolves it
breathing three-four time
and it's one two three
one two three
one

PART THREE: Waiting for the Season to Change

Rescue

I left the hospital
floating on a river
of hope
Radiant she was
New life in her eyes
expectations for
tomorrow
We have both been drowning
all winter
in icy waters of
inevitable loss
struggling up
again and again
until the answer seemed
just not to struggle
anymore

And then to be so suddenly
rescued,
to have another chance…
it is spring
and we can dream
and we can
float along the river
gently and easily
together for the voyage
yet awhile

Aufwiedersehen?

The first day of March
the last day of hearts
I'm missing already your eyes
I know how it is
I know how it was
I can't even change it with lies

Beginnings are hunger
endings last longer
I wish you sweet dreams in the night
Perhaps time will blind us
Perhaps we won't find us
but maybe, just maybe, we might

Rules Were Made to Be

She shouldn't have
She could have stopped
anywhere along the way
never let him inside
house
arms
lips
It was easy
after that
He followed her
to the river
night after night
week after we
Slivers of moonlight
caught between
ought to
and can't
Nobody knew
that they went there
Nobody knew
what they did
or how
once it started
she didn't care
about stopping
anywhere
along the way

Tourists that Maim

Enter the Kingdom
if you dare

Rental car breakers
shuttle bus bashers
and door that slam
bump in the night
Half-eaten suckers
back-handed slushers
popcorn that bursts into flight

Swords cut elastic
pistols flail plastic
balloons thump away
as they fight
Cap bills poke forward
feathers jab over
pith helmets try as they might

Strollers smash ankles
shoulders hold yankers
wheelchairs stub toes
that they sight
They all call it Disney
these shin kicks that dizzy
Mickey don't bark–
he just bites

Waiting for the Season to Change

Sunshine smiles down
while Douglas firs
and redwoods feel
the slice of dreams
A few more die
because you're there
and so do I
As many more are born again
and so are we?
Two stories echo without you
Two stories yearn to be told
I love you
so hard
to hear in the darkness
while I wait
for summer mornings
when sunshine
is certain
to smile down
on two

In Contempt?

Called to testify
a clever d.a.
faces off against
a simple farm wife
(or so he thought)

Madam, did you discuss this case
with anyone prior to today?
Yes, sir

And what did you say EXACTLY?
I'd rather not say, sir

Answer my question!
Your honor! Direct her to answer!

Go ahead, ma'am

Yes, your honor
Well, I said
if there were any questions
I didn't know how to answer...
Yes???

I could probably say
"I'm not sure..." or
Yes?!

"I don't know..."
Yes?!
but not...

Silence

Your honor!

Go on, ma'am

But not, "It beats
the shit out of me."

YOUR HONOR!!

A red-faced lawyer
a smug old woman
a grinning judge

Sorry, Mr. Prosecutor,
but you asked

Puppy Love

Little girl dog
smiles up with
dreamy brown eyes
You are everything
she says
snuggling warm
beside my legs
gentling me
into another day
She patters behind me
all loyalty
from bathroom to kitchen
to bedroom and back again
until finally I can delay
no longer
and turn to leave her
pacing about her kennel
for another ten hours
waiting, waiting
for my eventual return
and when at last I get there
do I see
anger?
resentment?
No, just
a little girl dog
smiling up

Behind the Clouds

The hand of God
is beckoning
or is He pointing?
Right direction
wrong direction
Have you hugged
your destiny today?
Can't see behind
the solid wall
accumulated nimbus
No Moses
I cannot part
this blue-gray sea
And so I wait
and wait
to meet tomorrow

Wisdom of an Unborn Child

In a dream
she warned that
she couldn't stay much longer
and then I would have to be
the part that lasts
Such responsbility
to carry on her darting eyes
cynical optimism
biting wit and intelligence
all alone
While she lives
I don't feel old enough
to be a mother
but when she dies
just how long can I remain
a daughter?
A tiny voice
from deep within
whispers
We could give her life
forever
Do you listen?
do you lessen?
or will you sing?

When a Friend is a Friend

Nothing but shadow
for so long
afraid of the dark
but lost in it anyway
looking back
looking black
swallowed up by
inky memories
and tentacled
unnamed fears
Everyone else
unnerved by the change
whispering all the while
stepping away with
both eyes fixed
on the madness
Everyone
except you
who struck a single
wooden match
long and bright enough
to burn the midnight

Start Your Engine?

Caught inside unlikely
possibilities
Probably won't
can't happen
but what if...
The dream is better
than the journey
Reality is a
rocky field of disappointments
but fantasy
an open policeless road
Here inside my head
the sun is bright
the destination clear
and the wheel
slides easy in my hand
To drive or not to drive
that is the question
on the magical mystery tour

Last Song of Spring

Everyone knows that
robins migrate
but never south
in summer
I can't bear to
watch you fly away to nest
taking the finest weather
with you
Maybe the sun will shine
and maybe the rains will be warm
but the loons will surely mourn
your leaving
and so will I
because June, July, August
and infinity
won't be the same
without Robin

Manhattan Diagram

You walked with me
on the island of the sun
beside a whistling melody
over rushing taxis
behind a trail of expensive colognes
You walked with me
on the island of the moon
into the lilting heart of Broadway
under a canopy of blue diamonds
out of and into the night
Prepositions defy distance
the object of my affection
separated only by
the length of the sentence

PART FOUR: The Summer of Fathers

Departure

The end is in sight–
we all can see it
We walked for a while
but the road's come undone
I squint at their faces;
they're all disappearing
Marching away
like the battle is won

Where are they going
and who will they meet?
What lies ahead
as this comes to an end?
Are they reflective
and sad to be going?
Are they ecstatic
to be rounding the bend?

What have they taken?
What have they given?
What have they learned
to set themselves free?
And when they are older
and settled, established,
what sorts of thoughts
will they think about me?

Next week looks hollow;
their laughter will echo
I will be watching them
taking their leave
One lonely woman
will hug at their shadows
look over her shoulder
and try to believe

Escaping Oz

Living inside of a whirlwind
Peace at the eye of the storm?
Who can survive a tornado?
Funnel's the deadliest form

Torn all apart by you ought to
Swallowed by clouds of you must
Do this and do that like they tell you
Then settle once more into dust

Control is the essence of living
Who tells the winds where to blow?
If there's any way out of the tempest
you've got to know which way to go

Setting Sail

My life has been a journey
upon an emerald sea
Sailing isn't easy
though a sailor I may be

Water churns from gray to blue
and back again to green
Storms and clouds and crashing waves
All this and more I've seen

The voyage isn't simple
but it hasn't yet been long
There's time enough to get it right
as well as get it wrong

Some vessels end up sinking
while others hug the shore
It's risky to haul cargo
It's risky to make war

Behind me fade the fearful ones
who never leave the land
They stand and look with longing
held captive by the sand

While I, I face the typhoon
set off once more for sea
Sailing isn't easy
but it's all there is for me

Metaphor

This morning
I sped by a
whitetail that
hadn't been so lucky
Front legs outstretched
still running
for the other side,
she lay frozen
in a position of
foiled escape
Brown eyes
a sweet face
almost in repose
It seemed I ought
to slow the moment
really look at
and honor the dead
but I was late
the clock was ticking
and I was running
To what?
To where?
Just eternity
with my own legs
still racing
towards the grave

Things My Father Taught Me

Hard work and energy
keep you thin
A grin can get you by
Live it like you mean it, girl
'cause when you die, you die

Polkas and game shows
make you laugh
Too much rots your mind
Cleverness dresses in denim and silk
The time you need you find

It's better to spend it
while you're young
than save it for when you're old
Nobody ever got rich from a farm
he lived on but never got sold

Far away places beckon in youth
Travel before you get tired
All that you see as you nap on the couch
are faces of children you sired

Still hard work and energy
sure keep you thin
and a grin can get you by
Live it like you mean it, girl
'cause when you die, you die

Cinderella

(Hangzhou, China, July 16, 1994)

On the sidewalk
drenched in warm rain
lies a white high-heeled shoe
No one seems to
even see it there
waiting, waiting
for a Chinese woman
whose feet will never be bound
to realize it has fallen
from her bag
and frantically retrace her steps
A week's wages
to lengthen her legs
to stretch the muscles in her calves
Of course it's worth it.
It's all she knows of hope
as she stands on tiptoe
reaching for a Western dream

Second

Mac, where have you seen
hair that color before?
she asked my father
His silence answered
but did not answer
her question
Don't you remember?
Look at it–just a
hint of red gleaming in all
that deep brown
and not a bit of gray
Don't you really
remember?
Yes, he muttered
behind his newspaper
as if to say
But we were all
younger then

I look at her now
True, only a trace
of brown dully
emerges from
tired
over-processed gray
but there I shine
before her
her face, her eyes, her hair
forty years ago
still beautiful
declaring a temporary truce
in the battle of age

Machtan's Corollary to Murphy's Law

Shouldn't
forbidden
taboo
cannot
you mustn't
you couldn't
you won't
Publicly
rules seem to
matter so much
In private
they do–
but
they don't

Empathy

The potentilla
are smacking their lips tonight
along with fleabane,
bougainvillea, and begonia,
plantain lilies, hollyhocks, and apple trees,
even two tiny experimental redwoods
lost in a tangle
of wild daisy.
Take a big, deep drink, I said,
all of you forgotten August babies.

How lucky for them that the sun
had beaten down so steadily
for of week of eighty plus,
that the water
splashed so cool
into the five-gallon bucket
against my face and legs,
and that my own
deep and dusty thirst
had been for much too long
unquenchable

The Summer of Fathers

Alarms shrilled
loud and long
He's not right,
Jan said–
it's starting again,
just like it did
with Mom
He doesn't remember
my phone number
Doesn't even know how
to look it up
Congestive heart failure
then nothing
The summer of fathers
6 a.m. phone call
Can you cover for Sue today?
Her father; heart attack;
twenty minutes ago;
fifty-eight.

The summer of fathers
Did you hear about Jack?
His father–nursing home
Doesn't want anyone to know
Psychologist
Janitor
Somebody
and somebody
and somebody
Death waltzes
with any partner
and you know
my father's always loved
to dance
I'm afraid to call home
afraid to ask.

The autumn equinox
September 22
Maybe then I can
breathe easier again

It Begins August First

"Ready to go back to school?"
they ask
with barely contained glee.

"I will be," I say,
"when it's time."

But it's not time YET.
Wisconsin summer
is at best an oxymoron.
How can they stand to end it
with four glorious weeks to go?
By Labor Day I will be ready
for yellow-orange school bus days
and crisp blue nights,
freshly-ironed blouse,
new skirt and sweater,
but for now it's
bare arms and legs,
hot sun baking me brown,
and warm breezes
kissing the nape of my neck.
It's still to soon
to end this love affair.
It's still to soon
to say goodbye to summer.

Cheek to Cheek

We have danced a thousand miles
since we entered here
We have waltzed through wind and rain
We have tangoed fear

Our future is a fox-trot
A samba is our past
We're two inside a ballroom
of partners meant to last

Just Desserts: A Delightful Mixture of Poems and Recipes by Darlene Machtan (2001)

In Appreciation

Ideas come from many places. The concept of combining poetry with recipes in this book sprang from two sources. An episode of *Newhart* has inspired countless "Poetry and Pastry" contests in my Creative Writing class; this book is much like the collection of recipes and poems that students produce to include at that reading/bake off. I hadn't seriously considered publishing such a book myself until I started doing book signings at local bookstores. Curious customers were often excited by the spiral bound chapbooks they saw before them until they learned that they were books of poems, not recipes. "Oh, darn," they'd say, "I was hoping it was a cookbook. I love cookbooks, but I hate poetry." So it occurred to me that since "a spoonful of sugar helps the medicine go down," perhaps it was time to merge the two genres. Hence, you have in your hands, *Just Desserts*, a book which combines my favorite dessert recipes and my favorite poems about people receiving exactly what they deserve.

I am unable to credit these recipes to any individuals or cookbooks. Like most cooks, I have boxes full of recipes that I have accumulated over the years from dozens of different sources that I have forgotten or lost touch with. And even if I knew whom the recipes came from originally, those people probably don't know where they got them either. Most of what I have included here I have also modified to suit my personal tastes and style. Many thanks to all the great anonymous dessert chefs who unknowingly contributed to this delicious collection.

Thanks also to the readers who helped choose the poems which appear here. Without Julie Bronson, Jane Roe, Marie Martini, Nan Andrews, Bob Heideman, and Jim Nuttall, I'd still be trying to decide what to include.

Finally, an enormous thank you to Jonna Jewell, whose computer expertise shaped this strange conglomeration into an attractive, readable, useful collection of what I hope is the best of me.

Food For Thought

In the dream
the sympathetic shrink
requests a recipe
that describes my life
This is easy, I say

First the ingredients:
One gallon vanilla ice cream
16 ounces of hot fudge
50 Maraschino cherries
1 quart of whipped cream

The directions:
Put all the cherries
on all the whipped topping
on all the hot fudge
smothering all the ice cream

Enjoy at once.

Not a bad recipe
on a smaller scale, he smiles
Nothing too complex or dangerous
It's the excessiveness
that causes the trouble
the fact that it's bigger than life
anybody's life
except yours
Too much too often
is poisoning you, he says.

He makes perfect sense, I realize
as I lie there curled up on my couch
and it didn't even cost me
fifty bucks an hour.

Chocolate Covered Cherries

1/3 cup softened butter
2 cups (1 jar) marshmallow cream
Dash of salt
1 teaspoon almond extract
4 cups, sifted, powdered sugar
60 Maraschino cherries (1½-2 10 ounce jars)
1 (12 ounce) package milk or semi-sweet chocolate chips

Cream butter. Beat in marshmallow cream, salt, and almond extract. Add sugar gradually, mixing well after each addition. Turn out and knead in powdered sugar, adding powdered sugar until mixture is no longer sticky.

Drain cherries thoroughly. Press thumb into 1" pieces of fondant and insert cherry in thumbprint. Wrap each cherry in fondant, being sure it is completely covered. Refrigerate overnight. Melt chocolate chips in small saucepan over very low heat. Remove from heat as soon as chips are melted.

Dip wrapped cherries in chocolate. Place dipped cherries on waxed paper and refrigerate to harden.

A Little Wind

blows through the corner wall
Candlelight flickers
and your eyes
wonder if I'm warm enough
A glass of some fine wine
(Maybe French, maybe Italian)
stands untouched
The crowded dance floor beckons
but the music is sweeter here
A man laden with six dozen red roses
stops to ask if
the lady would like one
and your eyes wonder
Yes, here, tonight,
alone with you,
I'm warm enough

Bon Bons

½ cup butter
3 cups finely chopped pecans
1 small package flaked coconut
1 can sweetened condensed milk
3 cups powdered sugar
1 teaspoon vanilla
2 (6 ounce) packages chocolate chips

Melt butter and pour over pecans. Add coconut, milk, sugar, and vanilla and mix well. Shape into 1" balls.

Melt chocolate chips in top of double boiler. Remove from heat when melted. Dip balls in chocolate and roll in powdered sugar.

And Now a Word From Your Sponsor

I exact this one promise
in setting you free
Plot your own course
don't do it for me

For father or mother
in spite of the same
Yesterday's over
It went as it came

You were thwarted by ill winds
colder than most
but the horizon is clearing
from here to the coast

Choose your direction
Move with the sun
Cruise strong and steady
but don't ever run

You can do anything
I've seen you do it
But you could do nothing
and forget that you knew it

Nobody's prouder
of you than I am
But now that it's over
it's out of my hands

I exact this one promise
in setting you free
Sail high as the moonbeams
Be all you can be

Rocky Road Fudge Bars

Batter
½ cup butter
1 square or 1 ounce envelope unsweetened chocolate
1 cup sugar
1 cup flour
1 teaspoon baking powder
1/2 cup chopped nuts
1 teaspoon vanilla
2 eggs

Filling
6 ounces cream cheese, softened
1/2 teaspoon vanilla
1/2 cup sugar
1/4 cup butter, softened
2 Tablespoons flour
1 egg
1/4 cups chopped nuts
2 cups mini marshmallows

Frosting
¼ cup butter
1 ounce unsweetened chocolate
2 ounces cream cheese
¼ cup milk
3 cups powdered sugar
1 teaspoon vanilla

Preheat oven to 350° F. In large saucepan, melt butter and chocolate over low heat. Remove from heat. Add sugar, flour, nuts, baking powder, vanilla, and eggs. Mix well. Spread in greased and floured 13" x 9" pan.

In a bowl, combine filling ingredients and spread over chocolate mixture in pan. Bake 25-35 minutes or until toothpick inserted in center is clean. Sprinkle marshmallows and bake 2 minutes longer.

Immediately prepare frosting by combining butter, chocolate, cream cheese, and milk in saucepan. Heat over low heat until chocolate melts. Stir in powdered sugar and vanilla until smooth. Pour over marshmallows and swirl together. Cool and cut into bars.

Yield: 36 bars.

Tip
Whenever chocolate chips are called for in any recipe throughout this book, use semi-sweet or milk chocolate

Lemon Bars

Crust:

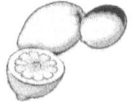

    ¾ cup butter
    1½ cups flour
    6 Tablespoons powdered sugar

Filling:

    4 eggs, beaten
    2 cups sugar
    ½ teaspoon salt
    4 Tablespoons flour
    6 Tablespoons lemon juice

Frosting:

    2 teaspoons grated lemon rind
    2 Tablespoons lemon juice
    1 cup powdered sugar

Mix together crust ingredients and spread in 13" x 9" pan. Bake at 350° F for 20 minutes.

Combine filling ingredients in a sauce pan, bring to a boil, and boil 1 minute. Cool. Spread on hot baked crust, and bake another 25-30 minutes.

Mix together frosting ingredients and frost while still warm.

Answering the Reproaches

You didn't warn us
that you were leaving
Nobody had a chance
to say all those unsaids
We need you
You changed us
There is no other
Love and love and more love
You just left

It rains a steady cold
today outside and
inside our hearts
There is no sunshine
at all and yet
your tree
on the front lawn
grows patiently and steadily
I'm still here
it quietly proclaims
bearing fruit
bearing witness
I didn't have to warn you
because I really
never left
at all

Basic Sweet Rolls Recipe

2 cups warm water
½ cup sugar
2 packages yeast
1 Tablespoon salt
6½ cups flour
2 eggs
½ cup vegetable oil

Cinnamon/Sugar Mixture
To ½ cup sugar,
add 2 teaspoons cinnamon
and mix well.

Stir sugar into warm water. Add yeast and allow to bubble a bit before adding salt. Add 2 cups of the flour and beat. Add the eggs and oil and beat until smooth. Add remaining 4½ cups of flour. The dough will be a bit thin. Brush top of dough lightly with oil, cover with waxed paper and a clean towel and allow to rise several hours until doubled in size.

After dough has risen, punch it down and roll it out on a floured surface into a rectangle. Spread generously with softened butter and sprinkle with cinnamon/sugar mixture. Roll up the dough and pinch the sides together.

Cut the dough in 1" slices. Place in greased 13" x 9" baking pan, cover with waxed paper and the towel again, and allow the dough to rise to top edge of pan. Bake at 375° F for about 20 minutes or until toothpick comes out clean and rolls are golden brown.

For frosted cinnamon rolls, simply let the rolls cool and frost with your favorite powdered sugar frosting. Add chopped nuts if desired.

For caramel pecan rolls:

Melt ½ cup butter in a 13" x 9" baking pan.
Remove from heat. Add 1 cup brown sugar and 2 Tablespoons corn syrup. Stir and evenly distribute the caramel mixture across the bottom of the pan. Sprinkle with chopped or halved pecans. Lay the slices of dough on top of the caramel mixture. Bake in the same way, but when done, loosen the edges of the rolls with a table knife, invert the pan onto cookie sheet or serving tray, and scrape extra caramel back onto the top of the rolls. Best when eaten warm.

Carrot Cake

2 cups sugar
1½ cups oil
4 eggs
2¼ cups flour
2 teaspoons salt
2 teaspoons baking soda
2 teaspoons cinnamon
3 cups grated carrots
1½ cups chopped nuts

Grease and flour 13' x 9" cake pan. Combine sugar, oil, and eggs, and beat 2 minutes. Sift dry ingredients together. Add to mixture and beat until smooth. Add carrots and nuts. Spread in pan. Bake at 300° F for 1 hour, until toothpick inserted in center comes out clean. Frost when cool.

Cream Cheese Frosting
8 ounces cream cheese
4 Tablespoons butter
2 teaspoons vanilla
4 cups powdered sugar

Cream together cream cheese, butter, and vanilla. Add powdered sugar and beat until smooth.

As September Leaves / Galaxy

As September Leaves

Orange bits of used-to-be
floating to the ground
Red pieces of my heart
dying without sound

Verdant promises of youth
yellowing with time
Growing up means growing old
the reason for the rhyme

Galaxy

Twinkling in your eyes
are the stars of your grandmother
your mother
your sisters
your sons
Generations:
God's constellations
that give the darkness magic
and your eyes a reason
to shine on

Frosted Pineapple Squares

½ cup sugar
3 Tablespoons cornstarch
¼ teaspoon salt
1 egg yolk, lightly beaten
1 can (1 pound 14 ounces) undrained, crushed pineapple

2/3 cup milk
1 teaspoon sugar
1 package yeast
¼ cup very warm water
4 egg yolks, beaten
4 cups sifted flour
1 cup butter

Make sauce of first five ingredients. Cool. Scald milk, add sugar and cool to lukewarm. Dissolve yeast in warm water and add to milk. Stir in eggs.

Measure flour into large bowl. Cut in butter until mixture is like coarse meal. Stir in yeast and milk. Blend well. Divide dough in half. Roll one half to fit 16" x 10" jelly roll pan. Top with sauce. Cover with other half of dough and seal edges. Snip top. Let rise until doubled in size. Bake at 375° F for 35 to 40 minutes. Frost with your favorite frosting.

A Wish and a Prayer

Somewhere
she rests
I hope it's warm there
and that she sips coffee
and forks through
a luscious plumcake
and smiles at lingering strangers

Somewhere
she nests
I hope they speak
a foreign foreign language
which she is
quick to master
I hope they don't ask
too much
or worse,
too little

Somewhere
she's blessed
Let there be
lost fathers and mothers
sisters and brothers
and dogs and
hibiscus, azalea, and roses
and her
let there be her
somewhere

Pie Crust/Blackberry Pie

2½ cups flour
2/3 cup shortening (lard is best)
½ to 1 teaspoon salt
Just enough water to moisten

Makes a generous amount for a two-crust pie with no problems rolling out.

For a blackberry pie, use 3½ cups blackberries, 1¼ cups sugar, 1/3 cup flour, ½ teaspoon cinnamon; lemon juice is optional. Dot with butter.

Bake in glass baking dish at 400° F for 35 to 50 minutes or until bubbly and crust is brown.

Tip
Go easy on the water—
add gradually
Too much...too late...too bad!

Berry Picking Primer

1. Record your soap opera—real life takes longer than expected.
2. Carefully choose one companion who can keep a secret. (I recommend a little white terrier.)
3. Carry a .44 only if you're willing to shoot the bear—a 3-pound pistol slows down a runner.
4. The harvest will be inversely proportional to the size of your chosen container.
5. Expect to be scratched, bitten and bruised.
6. The biggest berries required being pierced by the sharpest thorns.
7. Listen to the wind. Feel the sunshine. Ignore the mosquitoes.
8. Turn around—you may have just overlooked the bonanza.
9. Leave some behind for lost, hungry grandkids and other critters.
10. Don't be surprised if the picking is more satisfying than the pie.

Sugar Cookies

1 cup sugar
¾ cup butter
¼ cup milk
2 eggs
3 cups flour
3 teaspoons baking powder
¾ teaspoon salt
Flavor with vanilla, cinnamon, or nutmeg to taste

Cream sugar and softened butter. Stir in beaten eggs and milk. Add sifted flour, baking powder, salt, spices, and vanilla. Roll out on floured surface and cut out with cookie cutters. Bake at 375 until golden brown. Cool, frost, and decorate

Tip
Cover bowl with waxed paper and chill before rolling and cutting

Big Wheel of Love

ascends
fast
At the top
it's clean and beautiful
I can see everything
from up there
The wind blows warm
and pure
I become the sunshine
and my heart explodes
inside the rush
of the ride

Big wheel of love
descends
slowly
At the bottom
it is muddy and ugly
I am blind down there
covered and smothered by
the dirt we've both become
The tedium of our steady decline
collapses my eyes and dreams

until the big wheel
in its own time
and with the certainty of cycles
rises again

Wedding Cake Frosting

1 pound powdered sugar
½ cup Crisco®
2 egg whites
½ teaspoon almond extract
1 teaspoon vanilla extract

Combine ingredients and beat on medium speed until smooth.

Tip
For chocolate frosting, add 1/3 cup unsweetened cocoa

But Aren't You Married?

About to run away
again
I can't help it
Someone out there
keeps calling
some name
that I believe
belongs to me
Wife
Daughter
Teacher
A winter identity
but there is an
unencumbered summer girl
with the same set of
fingerprints
and a longing for
far away places, for laughter
He knows as I again depart
the certainty of
solid love and return
and leaving just one last time,
just one last time
to find me

Blond Brownies

2/3 cups butter
2 cups brown sugar
2 Tablespoons water
2 eggs
2 teaspoons vanilla

2 cups flour
1 teaspoon baking powder
¼ teaspoon soda
1 teaspoon salt
1 cup nuts
1 cup chocolate chips

Melt butter. Add brown sugar, water, eggs, and vanilla. Add dry ingredients and nuts. Pour into greased 13" x 9" pan. Sprinkle chocolate chips evenly over the top. Bake in 350° F oven for 20 to 25 minutes. Do not over bake.

Full Circle

He fell in love with the wrong woman
because her legs were perfect,
and she was quick to smile,
and she understood everything about him
before he said anything at all.
She fell in love with the wrong man
because his face was handsome,
and his eyes laughed,
and he gently held her secret self
in both his hands.
Love–

so the wrong one
became the right one, right then.
Maybe it should have been
someone else,
but it wasn't.
No, it isn't.
And now,
he has his business,
and she has her children,
and he doesn't listen
and she doesn't ask
and neither is certain how
or why or when
the right one
became the wrong one
once again.

Molasses Sugar Cookies

1½ cups shortening
2 cups sugar
½ cup molasses
2 eggs
4 cups flour
1 teaspoon salt
4 teaspoons soda
1 teaspoon cloves
1 teaspoon ginger
1 teaspoon cinnamon

Cream shortening and sugar. Add eggs and molasses and beat well. Sift dry ingredients and add to mixture.

Form into 1" balls and roll in sugar. Bake on greased cookie sheet at 375° F for 8 to 10 minutes.

So Far Away

Take me home to misty skies
take me home to blue
take me home to yesterday
take me home to you

I have traveled far and wide
I have crossed the sea
Danced the dance of foreign tongues
the ones that wait for me

Seems like I must leave each time
each time I want to stay
Seems like that I lose each time
a little of my way

After just a little while
every place is home
'til homesick is a state of mind
no matter where I roam

Even when I'm here again
there is where I dream
When I'm there it's somewhere else
I really want to be

so take me home to misty skies
take me home to blue
take me home to yesterday
take me home to you

Lemon JELL-O® Gelatin Cake

1 package lemon cake mix
1 small package lemon JELL-O® gelatin
4 eggs
¾ cup corn oil
1 cup water

½ cup lemon juice
2 cups powdered sugar

Mix ingredients well. Beat 2 to 3 minutes at medium speed. Pour into 13" x 9" cake pan. Bake at 350° F for 45 minutes. Remove from oven and immediately prick entire cake with a fork, thrusting fork all the way through.

Mix lemon juice and powdered sugar and pour over entire cake.

Let cool before cutting. Standing 24 hours makes it even better.

Variation:
Use white cake mix and cherry JELL-O® gelatin.

Gone to the Dogs

End of another
fifteen-hour Wednesday
dragging myself up
the steps
burdened by briefcase, knapsack
and gym bag
I shoulder open
the door to
brown eyes flashing
their usual happy greeting
curled tails wagging hello
and then a burst of cheerful
eager "I love you" howls
But something is wrong
with this picture
Behind the two
Akita heartbeats
and over the noise
I see and hear
another beast in love with my return–
you
ridiculously poised on hands and knees
tail wagging
bearded chin tilting to the
ceiling,
howling along with them
singing my praises
singing your love
They're mad for me
and clearly, clearly,
so are you

Pecan Puffs

2 cups butter
1½ cups powdered sugar
5 cups flour
Pinch of salt
2 teaspoons vanilla
2 cups ground pecans

Mix all ingredients together and form into 1" balls. Bake at 350° F for 8 to 10 minutes or until bottoms are golden brown. Roll in powdered sugar.

Tip
Soften butter in microwave to almost melted—makes shaping puffs into balls much easier

Halfway There

Half a journal.
Half a play.
Half a quarter.
Half a winter.
Or maybe a little more.
Halfway to summer.
Halfway to China.
Halfway to dreams.
Halfway to death.
Half-hearted.
Half-interested.
Half-witted.
Half-baked.
Half of who I am
on a magic day
Half of who I'm
yet to be.
A little more
than I was
A little less
than I'll see.
Here's a riddle—
Who is bigger:
One who is half of
herself alone
or half of two?
Does the lover's
power diminish
or increase by
the number
that she loves?
And can the sum
of her parts
ever be greater than
the whole?

Raspberry Truffles

1 (10 ounce) package raspberry flavored chocolate chips
4 ounces softened cream cheese
2 Tablespoons raspberry jam
1 teaspoon butter
1 (12 ounce) package chocolate chips, melted
White coating (optional)

Melt chips over very low heat. Remove from heat when melted. Add cream cheese, jam, and butter. Chill until firm enough to shape. Form into 1" balls and place on waxed paper-lined cookie sheet. Dip balls in chocolate and place on waxed paper to harden. If desired, melt white coating and drizzle over the truffles. Strawberry, lemon, orange, or peppermint variations can be made from the same recipe by altering jam and extract/liqueur flavors.

Tip
If raspberry chips aren't available, use regular chocolate chips with raspberry extract or liqueur, to taste

Historian

Out there
is my past somewhere
It follows me like
a shadow
emerging longer
in the evenings
Mornings I hardly notice
rarely look back
but on my 5 o'clock walks
it looms large and significant
before me, saying,
"You were
you could have,
you didn't."
Winter Novembers
turn everything to black
long before it's time
so I try to
fill the inside up
with candles
and burning embers
and the light of you
you, who illuminates
the shadows
and remembers
the best of who I was
and who I am

Ting A Lings

1 (12 ounce) package chocolate chips
1 (6 ounce) package butterscotch chips
2 cups peanuts (skinless)
2 cans (5½ ounces each) Chinese noodles

Melt together over barely boiling water (in a double boiler), chocolate chips and butterscotch chips. Add peanuts and Chinese noodles.

Drop by teaspoonfuls on waxed paper.

Intolerance

I said what I meant
I meant what I said
but you only hear what you hear
Nothing but static
Nothing but white noise
What is it, my friend, that you fear?

Your eyes are so blue
and mine are so brown
you can't even see what I see
Blinded by contrast
and blinded by self
You don't even know that I'm me

Different, not deviant
Unlike, not unfit
I am what I am, just like you
You could have been me
so you'd better remember
I am somebody too

Cherry Walnut Coffee Cake

5 to 5½ cups flour
¼ cup sugar
1 teaspoon salt
1 teaspoon grated lemon peel
2 packages dry yeast

½ cup water
1 cup milk
2 sticks butter
2 eggs
2 cups chopped walnuts

2/3 cup chopped Maraschino cherries
3 Tablespoons sugar

In large bowl, mix 2 cups flour, ¼ cup sugar, salt, lemon peel, and yeast. Combine milk, water and butter in saucepan. Heat over low heat until very warm. Butter need not melt.

Gradually add to dry ingredients and beat 2 minutes. Add eggs and ½ cup flour. Beat 2 minutes. Stir in enough additional flour to make a stiff dough. Cover bowl. Set aside 20 minutes. Combine 2 Tablespoons sugar, walnuts, and cherries.

Divide dough in half. Roll out each half into 14" x 10" rectangle. Spread with filling. Roll up from long side. Cut diagonal slits every inch.

Pull cut pieces alternately left and right. Brush with oil. Cover and refrigerate 2 to 24 hours. Let stand 10 minutes out of refrigerator before baking.

Bake at 375° F for 25 to 30 minutes. Frost with powdered sugar frosting. Garnish with cherries and nuts.

Butterscotch Supreme Dessert

Crust:

> ½ stick butter
> ½ cup flour
> 1 Tablespoon sugar

Filling:

> 4 ounces cream cheese
> ½ cup powdered sugar
> ½ cup whipped topping

Topping:

> 1 small package instant butterscotch pudding
> 1½ cups cold milk
> toasted coconut
> ¼ cup pecans

Mix together crust ingredients and press into 8" x 8" pan. Bake at 350° F for 15 minutes.

Combine filling ingredients and spread on cooled crust.

Mix together pudding and milk and pour onto filling layer. Top with additional whipped topping. Garnish with toasted coconut and pecans.

Just Desserts

Eyes meeting over menus
impossible to choose
"You decide"
Intoxicating
unaccustomed liquered fruit
Drunk on
something for which
there is no proof
Stay or go
go or stay
Impossible to choose
Die Rechnung, bitte

In the end
you pay for
the sweetest treats
and you can't remain
in a sidewalk café forever
even if you're gliding
through a holiday
on eis

Rhubarb Dessert

First layer:

    3 cups chopped rhubarb
    1½ cups sugar
    1 Tablespoon flour

Second layer:

    ¾ cup brown sugar
    ¾ cup oatmeal
    1 cup flour
    ½ cup butter

Combine first layer and put into 8" x 8" cake pan.

Mix together second layer and sprinkle over first layer and pat down.

Bake at 350° F for 40 minutes.

"Lights Out, Uh Huh—Flash, Flash, Flash"

I'm having a
hard time
looking at him
without grinning
Every night
it's a new scene
a little nastier
than the one before
Thought my rep
was ruined until
I realized
it was all a
MMMMMMmmmmmmmmmmmmm
dreamy
the way you can
get away with anything
in the privacy
of your own mind
unless
of course
you talk in your sleep

Chocolate Bars

Batter:

¼ cup cocoa
1 cup butter
1 cup water

2 cups flour
2 cups sugar
¼ teaspoon salt

½ cup buttermilk
2 eggs
1 teaspoon soda
1 teaspoon vanilla

Frosting:

½ cup butter
¼ cup cocoa
6 Tablespoons milk
1 pound powdered sugar
1/8 teaspoon salt
1 teaspoon vanilla

Combine cocoa, butter, and water in a large 2-quart saucepan and bring to a boil. Add flour, sugar, and salt, and mix well.

Add buttermilk, eggs, soda, and vanilla and beat until well blended. Pour into large jelly roll pan and bake at 400° F for 18 to 20 minutes.

Five minutes before cake is done, bring to a boil first three frosting ingredients (butter, cocoa, milk). Remove from heat and add remaining frosting ingredients (powdered sugar, salt, vanilla). Beat thoroughly and spread on cake while hot.

Hint: 1 pound powdered sugar = 3 cups.

Paradoxes

White rain
blue tears
colors that are inside out
and backwards
Nobody said I should love you
There can be no result
you said
but you were wrong
I wake up laughing
or cry in my sleep
and hold a secret
tightly in my empty hand
Everything and nothing
has changed
Everything and nothing
is who we are
The dark white world outside
is unable to choose
between your rain and my snow
as I promise
that this day by night
I will end it
just so we can both
begin again

Chocolate Mayonnaise Cake

1 cup sugar
1 cup mayonnaise
1 teaspoon vanilla
2 cups flour
2 teaspoons soda
4 level Tablespoons cocoa
1 cup cold water

Cream together sugar, mayonnaise, and vanilla. Sift three times: flour, soda and cocoa.

Add flour mixture to creamed mixture alternately with cold water. End with flour mixture. Beat well. Pour into 13" x 9" cake pan and bake at 350° F for about 25 minutes.

Prophecy

I come from the land of filet–
mignon, fish, even chicken
Where I live
we demand comfort and convenience
The land of filet
is a lifetime away
in a place where
they squat over holes to shit
in a place they launder
on a stone slab with
a bar of soap
in a place where they
chew around fish bones and frog bones
and bird bones
then carry their bowls
to a hot tiny room
that sleeps six
They expect little
They demand nothing
but they have heard stories
about the land of filet
and I believe
that if they choose
they will easily
chew it up
and spit it out–
those one billion people
who know exactly how
to eat around the bones

Peanut Butter Balls

2 cups (18 ounces) creamy peanut butter
½ cup butter
3 cups Rice Krispies® cereal
1 pound powdered sugar (3 cups)
Chocolate chips, melted

Crush Rice Krispies®. Melt peanut butter and butter. Add cereal and powdered sugar. Form into small balls.

Melt chocolate chips over very low heat stirring constantly. Remove from heat as soon as chocolate is melted.

Dip balls in melted chocolate. Put dipped peanut butter balls on waxed paper to harden. When hard, package in moisture and vapor-proof containers.

Reality Check

Always
Forever
Temporarily
Never
A hundred diamond rings
in one hundred thousand
pawnshops
ten million broken promises
Nineteen-years old
Just married
but they had a fight
so she stabbed him
in the stomach
with a handy kitchen knife
lying next to the Minute Rice

Or how about the guy
who found his wife
of four years in bed
with another man
and the judge said
he had every right to
nearly kill her
Not a man alive
could walk away from that

Wedding dresses
two for a dollar
at garage sales
Silk bouquets
so she can carry them again
Forsaking all others
'til death do us part
Yeah, right

Black Forest Cake

Main ingredients:
2 eggs (separate whites and yolks)
¾ teaspoon soda
1 teaspoon salt
1 cup milk
2 (1 ounce) squares unsweetened chocolate, melted and cooled
1½ cups sugar
1¾ cups sifted cake flour
1/3 cup salad oil
2 pints whipping cream

Cherry filling:
1 (1 pound, 4 ounces) can pitted, tart, red cherries, drained
½ cup port wine
1 Tablespoon kirsch
3 drops almond extract

Chocolate mousse:
3 (1 ounce) squares semisweet chocolate
1 cup whipping cream
3 Tablespoons kirsch
1 egg, well beaten
2 Tablespoons sugar

Butter frosting:
6 Tablespoons butter
Light cream (about ¼ cup)
1½ teaspoons vanilla
1 (1 pound) package powdered sugar, sifted (3 cups)

Directions:

> **Cherry filling**–Combine all ingredients and chill 3 to 4 hours or overnight. Drain thoroughly.

Chocolate mousse—Combine chocolate and kirsch in top of double boiler; stir over hot (not boiling) water until chocolate melts and mixture is smooth. Slowly stir in 1 well-beaten egg. Whip 1 cup whipping cream and 2 tablespoons sugar; fold into chocolate. Chill 2 hours.

Black Forest Cake—Beat 2 egg whites until soft peaks form. Gradually add ½ cup sugar, beating until stiff peaks form. Sift together sifted cake flour, 1 cup sugar, soda, and salt into mixing bowl. Add salad oil and ½ cup milk. Beat 1 minute on medium speed on electric mixer. Scrape bowl often.

Add ½ cup milk; 2 egg yolks, and unsweetened chocolate, melted and cooled. Beat one minute longer, scraping bowl frequently. Gently fold in egg whites. Pour into two greased and lightly floured 9" round pans. Bake in moderate oven (350° F) for 30 to 35 minutes. Cool 10 minutes; remove from pans. Cool thoroughly. Split each layer in half making 4 layers. Set aside.

Butter Frosting—Cream butter; gradually add about half the sugar, blending well. Beat in 2 tablespoons cream and vanilla. Gradually blend in remaining sugar. Add enough cream for spreading consistency. Frosts two 8" or 9" layers.

To Assemble:
Spread ½ cup butter frosting on the cut side of a cake layer. With remaining frosting, form one ridge ½" wide and ¾" high around outside edge of same cake layer. Make another ridge 2" from outside edge. Chill in freezer for 30 minutes, shaping intermittently.

Fill space with Cherry Filling. Spread second cake layer with Chocolate Mousse and place unfrosted side atop first. Chill in freezer for 30 minutes.

Whip 2 cups whipping cream with 2 tablespoons sugar and 1 teaspoon vanilla. Spread third cake layer with 1½ cups whipped cream and place atop second layer. Top with fourth cake layer.

Frost top layer and sides of cake with remaining whipped cream. Garnish with Maraschino cherries and chocolate curls. Chill for 2 hours.

September Song

Come here,
old girl,
Let's watch
the turning
burning leaves
and geese flying
away from us
once again
The lake shimmers
gray today
but your eyes
are still blue
Mostly we sit
and look out now
and we remember
You were in such
a hurry then
To get here?
Give me your gnarled hands
I will hang on
to them
as long as there
is autumn
and you

Friendship Brownies

½ cup walnuts
½ cup vanilla chips
½ cup chocolate chips
2/3 cup brown sugar
2/3 cup flour
1/3 cup cocoa
1/3 cup sugar
½ cup + 2 Tablespoons flour
¾ teaspoon salt
1 teaspoon baking powder

Layer the ingredients in the order given in a quart-sized mason jar. Attach a note with the following:

> To this mixture, in a large bowl, add 3 eggs, 2/3 cup oil, and 1 teaspoon vanilla.
> Mix all ingredients together and pour into a greased 13" x 9" pan. Bake at 350° F for about 25-30 minutes.

Ticked Off

Why is it
sixteen year olds
have so much of you
to waste
and I
have none at all?
Is it because
they are young enough
and fast enough
to catch you
while I labor
just to stay behind?
Does their clock
have more hours
and their calendar
more pages
because I have already
spent more than twice my share?
Or is it just a
cruel law of nature
that the ones who
need the least
are granted the most?
I'd explore it,
but, as usual,
I'm out of time.

Sorcery

September leaves just beginning to turn
But inside they have been brown and wrinkled
for a long, long time
I sit before them
suddenly much younger than
my almost forty years
conjuring memories
with an accordion
its reedy voice casting a spell of yesterday
Some find words to once familiar
Irving Berlin
A Pretty Girl Is Like a Melody
Marie
Remember?
I'll Be Loving You Always
They sway
They clap and tap
They moan
while two are weeping softly
An hour-long return to youth
and then I close the case
They stare in resignation
at age spots, iron chairs and institution tile
I'll come again, I promise
but I wonder
just how wise it is to conjure such a spell

Final Tip

Other Books by Darlene Machtan

Conversations With My Mother
Daddy's Long Goodbye

Machto Publishing

About the Author

Darlene Machtan's poetry has appeared in five editions of *The Wisconsin's Poet's Calendar*. Between 1988 and 2001 she published three chapbooks of poetry. Her memoir *Conversations With My Mother* was released in 2004 and its companion piece *Daddy's Long Goodbye* in 2020. She is a daughter, sister, writer, teacher, and friend. She lives in Northern Wisconsin with her husband, three dogs, and words that keep swirling in her head.

Title Index

A
Advice to the Adviser, 56
The American Pastime, 68
And Now a Word From Your Sponsor, 155
And They're Not Telling, 83
Answering the Reproaches, 159
Art Imitating Life, 65
"As If You Could Kill Time Without Injuring Eternity" (Henry David Thoreau), 70
As September Leaves, 163
Auction, 37
Aufwiedersehen?, 116
August in January, 104

B
Behind the Clouds, 123
Berry Picking Primer, 167
Big Wheel of Love, 169
Bill of Sale, 32
But Aren't You Married?, 171
But Is Anybody Listening?, 89
But It Will Never Happen to Me, 93

C
Calendar Girl, 105
"Cat's in the Cradle..." (Harry Chapin), 41
Cha lie's Ba 'n Grill, 59
Cheek to Cheek, 143
Cinderella, 136

D
The Day After, 103
Dealing With It, 110
Deluge, 95
Departure, 131
Depth Perception, 50
Double Standards, 49
Driver's Education, 44

E
Eat My Words, 90
Empathy, 139
Empty, 102
Escaping Oz, 132
Eulogy, 36
Euthanasia, 52
Evolution, 14

F
Fall from Grace, 13
Falling Out, 67
February 14, 2142, 107
Fighting the Wizard of Is, 15
Final Tip, 203
Fires that Rage, 61
Fish Story, 66
Food for Thought, 151
For Laura, 51
For the Study Lab Boy, 45
Forecast, 87
Full Circle, 173

G
Galaxy, 163
"Gee, It's Great to Be...", 34
Gone to the Dogs, 177
The Grand Canyon, 98
Grave Robbery, 111

H
Halfway There, 179
Hell, 60
Historian, 181

I
In Contempt?, 120
In the Middle of Time Gone By, 5
Intolerance, 183
It Begins August First, 142

J
Just Desserts, 187

K
Knight Errant, 28

L
Last Song of Spring, 127
"Lights Out, Uh Huh—Flash, Flash, Flash", 189
A Little Wind, 153
Lost Inside Yesterday, 108
Love Poem, 82

M
Machtan's Corollary to Murphy's Law, 138
Manhattan Diagram, 128
Marriage is a Rugged Country, 12
Masterpieces, 88
Mentor, 47
Metaphor, 134
Missing You, 94

Momentum Meets Inertia, 16
Monday Blues, 46

N
Night Shift, 26
No Escape, 20

O
October Snow, 86
Open Heart, 35
Over Easy, 109

P
Paradoxes, 191
Phenomenon of the Tumorous Bed, 84
Piquancy, 53
Prophecy, 193
Puppy Love, 122

R
Re-cycling, 27
Reality Check, 195
Rescue, 115
Rules Were Made to Be, 117

S
Sabotage, 40
Season of Schizophrenia, 97
Second, 137
Seductress Interruptus, 19
September Song, 199
Setting Sail, 133
Sex in the '80s, 63
Six More Weeks of Winter, 48
Snow Ball, 112
So Far Away, 175
Sorcery, 202
Start Your Engine?, 126
The Summer of Fathers, 140

T
Telephone Telepathy, 18
Things My Father Taught Me, 135
This Time Yesterday, 43
Three Years from Retirement, 92
Ticked Off, 201
Time Travel, 106
Timing Is Everything, 96
Too Expensive, 22
Tourists that Main, 118
Two Below Zero, 24
Two for the Price of One, 54

V
Vicious Circle, 64

W
Waiting for the Season to Change, 119
Waking Alone at Midnight, 23
Weekend Pass, 38
What I Can't Remember, 71
Whatever Happened to the Future Farmers of America, 31
When a Friend is a Friend, 125
Winter Dreams, 101
Wisdom of an Unborn Child, 124
A Wish and a Prayer, 165
Write a Dream, 62

Recipe Index

B
bars:
   Chocolate, 190
   Lemon, 158
   Rocky Road Fudge, 156-157
Basic Sweet Rolls Recipe, 160-161
Black Forest Cake, 196-198
Blackberry Pie, 166
Blond Brownies, 172
Bon Bons, 154
brownies:
   Blond, 172
   Friendship, 200
Butterscotch Supreme Dessert, 185

C
cake:
   Black Forest, 196-198
   Carrot, 162
   Cherry Walnut Coffee, 184-185
   Chocolate Mayonnaise, 192
   Lemon JELL-O Gelatin, 176
Caramel Pecan Rolls, 161
Carrot Cake, 162
cereal, Rice Krispies®, in Peanut Butter Balls, 194
cherries:
   in Chocolate Covered Cherries, 152
   in Black Forest Cake, 196-198
   in Coffee Cake, Cherry Walnut, 184-185

Cherry Walnut Coffee Cake, 184-185
chinese noodles, in Ting A Lings, 182
chocolate chips:
   in Blond Brownies, 172
   in Bon Bons, 154
   in Chocolate Covered Cherries, 152
   in Friendship Brownies, 200
   in Peanut Butter Balls, 194
   in Raspberry Truffles, 180
   in Ting A Lings, 182
cocoa:
   in Chocolate Bars, 190
   in Chocolate Mayonnaise Cake, 177
   in Friendship Brownies, 185
Chocolate Bars, 175
Chocolate Covered Cherries, 152
Chocolate Mayonnaise Cake, 192
Coffee Cake, Cherry Walnut, 184-185
coconut:
   in Bon Bons, 154
   in Butterscotch Supreme Dessert, 186
cookies:
   Molasses Sugar, 174
   Sugar, 168
Cream Cheese Frosting, 162

D
Dessert:
   Butterscotch Supreme, 186

Rhubarb, 188

F
Friendship Brownies, 200
Frosted Pineapple Squares, 164
frosting:
    Cream Cheese, 162
    Wedding Cake, 170
Fudge Bars, Rocky Road, 156-157

L
lemon:
    in Cherry Walnut Coffee Cake, 184-185
    in Lemon Bars, 158
    in Lemon JELL-O® Gelatin Cake, 176
    truffles, 180

M
marshmallow:
    cream, in Chocolate Covered Cherries, 152
    minis, in Rocky Road Fudge Bars, 156-157
mayonnaise, in Chocolate Mayonnaise Cake, 192
Molasses Sugar Cookies, 174

P
peanut(s):
    in Peanut Butter Balls, 194
    in Ting A Lings, 182
pecan(s):
    in Pecan Caramel Rolls, 161
    in Pecan Puffs, 178
        in Bon Bons, 154

in Butterscotch Supreme Dessert, 186
pie:
    blackberry, 166
    crust, 166
pineapple, in Frosted Pineapple Squares, 164
pudding, in Butterscotch Supreme Dessert, 186
Puffs, Pecan, 178

R
Raspberry Truffles, 180
Rhubarb Dessert, 188
Rice Krispies® cereal in Peanut Butter Balls, 194
Rocky Road Fudge Bars, 156-157
rolls:
    Basic Sweet, 160
    Caramel Pecan, 1161

S
Squares, Frosted Pineapple, 164
Sugar Cookies, 168
    Molasses, 174

T
Ting A Lings, 182
truffles:
    Raspberry, 180
    Peanut Butter Balls, 194

W
walnuts:
    in Cherry Walnut Coffee Cake, 184-185
    in Friendship Brownies, 200
Wedding Cake Frosting, 170

www.ingramcontent.com/pod-product-compliance
Lightning Source LLC
Chambersburg PA
CBHW061217070526
44584CB00029B/3868